FROM Factory FLOOR TO Dance FLOOR

GUILDHALL PRESS

Published in December 2016 by
GUILDHALL PRESS
Ráth Mór Centre
Bligh's Lane
Derry
Northern Ireland
BT48 0LZ
T: (028) 7136 4413 – www.ghpress.com

ISBN 978 1 911053 21 7

This publication was developed in association with Creggan Enterprises and the Hive Studio at Ráth Mór, Creggan (www.hivestudio.org)

A CIP record for this book is available from the British Library.

Dedication to the Derry factory girls

*They sweated and sewed, they laughed
and cried, they brought hope and
happiness into the homes of Derry.*

About The Authors

Both Willie Deery and Patrick Durnin have had books published by Guildhall Press and plays performed recording and dramatising aspects of Derry's social history.

In his publication *Springtown Camp*, Willie Deery highlights the housing injustices within the city after WWII and the protests that eventually brought justice and equality. The story was performed as a drama production in Derry's Millennium Forum. In *Derry's Dance Halls of Romance*, Deery recalls 'The Boy Meets Girl' era of the showband scene.

Durnin's publication *The Famine and the Workhouse in Derry* records the catastrophe of the failure of the potato crop in Ireland in the mid-19th century and the British Government's inadequate relief measures. It was also produced as *The 13 Steps* in Derry's Playhouse. His *Tillies* publication, which detailed the history of the city's shirt industry, was also produced as a docu-drama in the Millennium Forum.

Acknowledgements

This account of the lives of the Derry factory girls on the factory floor and dance floor between the 1940s and the 1960s was to be written originally by author and local historian Willie Deery who had collected a large amount of first-hand reminiscences and photographs from the workers themselves over many months. Unfortunately, other commitments prevented Willie from achieving his long-held goal by himself and he unselfishly contributed his research to ensure this important story could be told. I was able to source some additional information and new imagery which I amalgamated with some extracts from my *Tillies* book (Guildhall Press, 2005) to complete the work.

To all those, ex-factory workers or otherwise, who gave of their time and shared their memories and photos with Willie and myself, a sincere thank you is given: Isobel Doherty, Clare Bridge, Mary White, Mary Harrigan, Irene McCarron, Mary McCallion, Anne Harkin, Sarah Moore, Lily Mallon, Sadie Morris, Stella McDaid, Eithne Duffy, Bridget Doherty, Mary Lynch, Mary McCloskey, Bridie Cooke, Margaret Nelis, Maisie McLaughlin, Phyllis McCourt, Kathleen Duffy, Berna McDermott, Mary Doherty, Louise Walsh, Marilyn McLaughlin, Phil Cunningham, Eddie Davis, Ronnie Simpson, Robert Ferris, Sean McLaughlin and the *Derry Journal*. Apologies to any contributor who may have been inadvertently omitted.

I am grateful to three authors whose work in particular proved invaluable in researching this publication. Harry McCourt's captivating *Oh How We Danced* (Guildhall Press, 1992) was very helpful in describing the local dance scene during the relative time periods covered. Willie Deery's wonderful *Derry's Dance Halls of Romance* (Guildhall Press, 2011) was also very informative about this exciting musical era. *The History of the Clothing Industry in Derry* by Professor Robert Gavin, first published in *Fabrics & Fabrication* (Context Gallery, 2001), provided some excellent reference material on the development, growth and eventual decline of the city's shirt industry. My sincere appreciation for their dedication to recording relevant aspects of the social and economic history of Derry which I have been able to draw on.

Working with the Guildhall Press staff of Paul, Joe, Declan, Peter, Kevin and Jim was very informal, informative and extremely helpful.

I would also like to thank my wife Mary and children Louise, Mary, Ciaran and Ronan for their encouragement.

A final richly deserved thank you to Willie Deery for his generous and important contribution to this publication. Hopefully the finished work reflects the original ambitions of Willie for the book and gives an insight into the life and times of the girls who toiled by day in difficult conditions on the factory floor and who took to the dance floor at the weekends in the numerous venues that sprang up in and around the city, all the while striving to support their families and better their lives during uncertain times.

Patrick Durnin
November 2016

Contents

Introduction   9

The Factory Horn Calling   12

Factory Stories   15

   Mary Harrigan   15

   Mary White   19

   Irene McCarron   21

   Mary McCallion   23

   Clare Bridge   26

Working Together and Wee Buns   28

Dancing Days and the 'Bars'   42

Twist and Shout   51

Factory Queen Dances   58

Romance and Rituals   65

Helping Hands   68

Happy Days and Annual Outings   69

Changing Times   78

Memories of Tillie's by Patrick Durnin   80

A Fitting Tribute   84

Epilogue   89

Archive Gallery   94

Factory Reunion Gallery   109

Introduction

The younger generation walking the streets of Derry today would probably not be aware of the significant era of social history represented by the various former large factory buildings they pass across the city which stand as a memorial and testament to the sewing skills of the city's shirt-factory girls. That history recorded the evolution from the hand-sewn shirt to the machine-stitched modern garment, from the fireside shirt-making tradition initiated by William Scott to a factory industry.

William Scott (inset) was a County Derry man from Balloughry and a weaver by trade who recognised the potential of an abundant female labour force skilled in the art of needlework that was associated with the cottage industries of 'sprigging' and embroidery. Scott set up a network of 'outworkers', women who sewed the component parts of the shirts in their homes. He would then collect the finished garments and send them off to Scotland, and later London, for onward distribution. William Scott was undoubtedly the founding father of shirt making in the city, for his embryonic shirt trade evolved into Derry's greatest industry.

It was an evolution that put Derry on the industrial map and reversed the traditional roles within family life as mothers and daughters took on the role of breadwinner in a city plagued with male unemployment.

It was at the end of the 19th century that the large purpose-built shirt factories began to appear on the city landscape, giving birth to Derry's shirt industry and the factory girls. Those Victorian factories – with their dull, drab and depressing working environment – evolved into more welcoming surroundings that catered for the social, economic and emotional needs of the 20th-century factory girl.

Factory horns became the cultural, social and economic identity of the city and also its alarm clock, for their soundings gave warning to the hundreds of women and young girls that time was running out for them to get into their work. At their machines they sewed and sang during the day and danced and dated at night in the many small and large dance halls, particularly during the late 1940s–60s, the years that this publication mostly relates to. Those years could be described as the 'golden years', when the shirt factories and dance halls were flourishing, particularly during the 'Jitterbug' era introduced by the American navy and during the 'swinging sixties'. During that era, the factory floor and the dance floor became intertwined with the working and social lives of the Derry shirt-factory girls.

Unfortunately for the city, the shirt-making era has passed into the history books and those large factory buildings that are still standing have taken on different social and economic functions as retail outlets and apartments. Many studies and publications have since been recorded and have produced a great volume of statistics documenting, describing and detailing Derry's shirt industry. But little has been written about the personal working lives of the factory girls whose contribution to the city's social and economic life was substantial and significant.

Fortunately, daily life and working conditions in the shirt factories during their heyday are very fondly and vividly remembered by today's grandmothers and mothers whose accurate and authentic reminiscences capture the atmosphere of what working in the factories was like. Only those who lived the story can tell the story. Hopefully, their reminiscences, which have remarkable similarities, will provide a true-to-life picture of the unique working life of the Derry factory girls that lies hidden behind the impersonal statistics of the history books. Some of those interviewed wished to remain anonymous and this publication has respected this request; it does not detract from the authenticity and impact of their stories.

Many of the former shirt factory buildings that are still standing have taken on different social and economic functions as retail outlets and apartments such as (above) Lloyd, Attree & Smith Factory on Great James Street and (below) the Star Factory on Foyle Road.

The Factory Horn Calling

The story of the Derry factory girls began with the opening of the first purpose-built shirt factory of Tillie and Henderson on Abercorn Road/ Foyle Road in December 1856. This was the start of an industry that grew for almost 150 years and created a lasting tradition among the female population of the city which brought thousands of women and young girls together to make shirts.

Summoned to work by the sound of the factory horn, they did so in groups with their arms linked, an outward sign of the closeness and

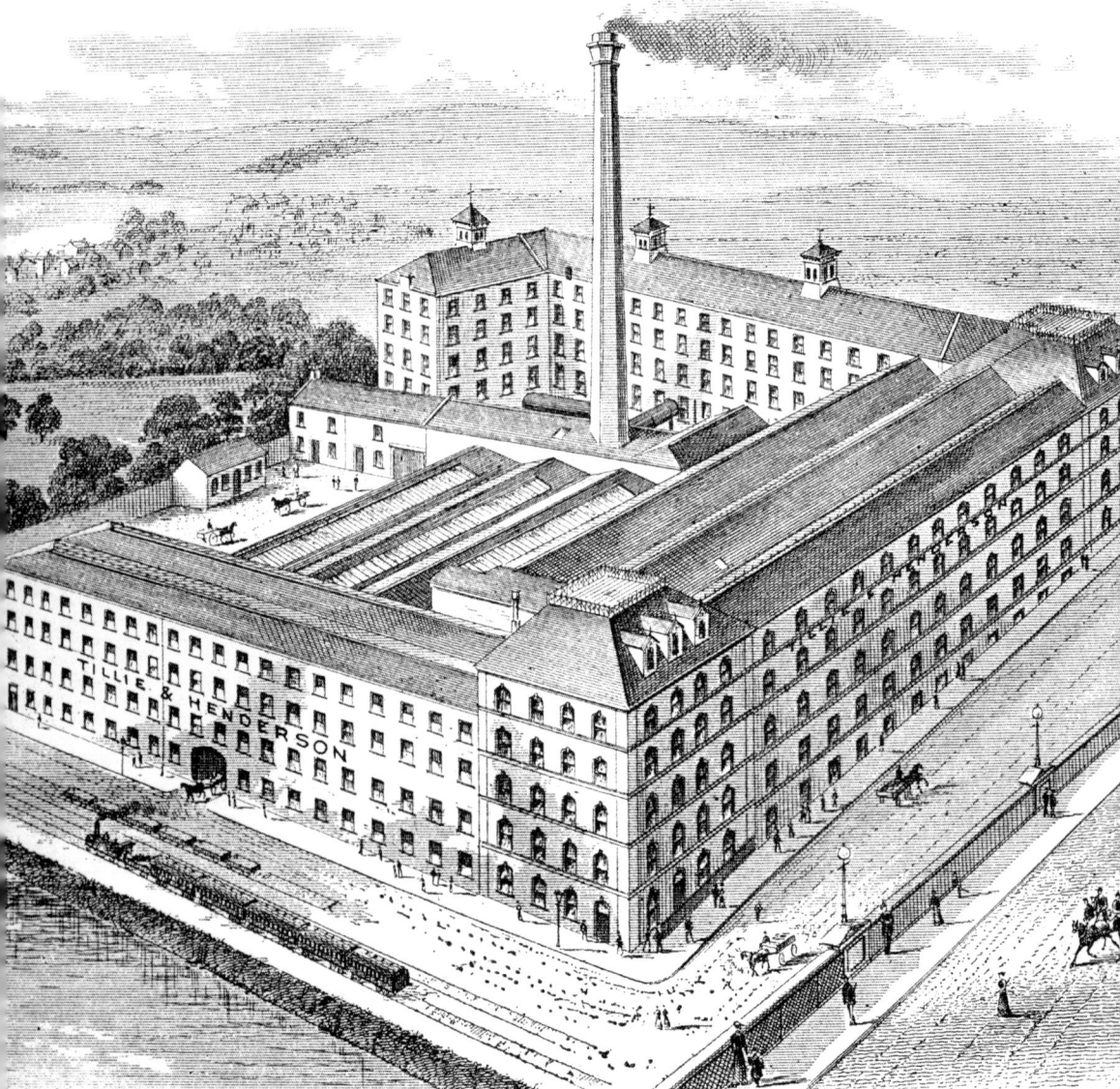

companionship among the factory girls down the decades. This continued inside the factory where they worked along both sides and length of the conveyor belt and on the 'line' at individual machines beside and behind each other. The linked-arm formation was quickly broken as the latecomers, prompted by the wailing factory horn, hurried to get into their work before the front doors closed at eight o'clock. Many of the girls who were 'locked out' would return home to face the music of a possible lecture from their mothers on the loss of a half-day's wages. Some girls would stand outside in the hope that some of the supervisors or departmental managers would recognise their 'key' workers and allow them in. Others, determined to get into their work, would exploit all possible entry points such as through the yard in Tillie's and up the back stairs, which many girls risked. The braver ones would take their chance that the general manager wasn't in the office and attempt that direct method of entry.

Scarves on, arms linked, and off to work.

On a memorable occasion, one inventive girl staged an outdoor activity scene to get into her work. Berna McDermott (née McShane), a hemmer in Tillie's, explains:

> Joan Kennedy, who was something of a personality, was locked out so she went into the children's play park beside the factory and started sliding down the banana slide and waving to all the girls in the factory who were looking out at her. So Davy (the factory manager) sent a girl out to bring her in, for there was no work being done.

To solve the problem of latecomers, the City Factory operated the quarter-hour policy that allowed the doors to re-open fifteen minutes after

Joan Kennedy.

eight o'clock and again at half past. This was a more subtle move by management that ensured that all the 'key' workers got to their machines.

Getting into work too early – particularly on Monday mornings – could be scary, as the rats, which were permanent residents of all shirt factories, had the freedom of the premises over the weekends and would be out on an early-morning stroll of their favourite picnic areas around the girls' machines before the conveyor belt was switched on. Since factory canteens were slow to be introduced, the girls had their tea breaks at their machines and all sorts of food crumbs would litter the floor, which made a change from the cloth and paper wrappings that were the factory rats' main menu. Kathleen Duffy, a patent turner in Tillie's, recalls:

When the cry 'Rats!' was heard, some girls would stand up on their stools to be safe and on one occasion Celine Clark, a hemmer, thought she would be safe standing on the conveyor belt only to see a rat running down the belt towards her. Both jumped off the belt at the same time. Some rats even had their own sleeping arrangements as Annie Doherty found out when she pulled out her drawer (attached to the machine for holding personal items) and a rat jumped out. She nearly brought the place down around her with panic.

Lloyd, Attree & Smith workers take time out for the camera. Included: Willie Long (department manager) and Anna McLaughlin.

Factory Stories

With the strong shirt-making culture in the city, the shirt factories were seen as an extension of the home and it was inevitable that many young school leavers were destined to follow their grannies, mammies and older sisters into one of the many factories. This life-changing role gave them an adult identity and created various emotions of nervousness, excitement, apprehension, and a sense of responsibility.

The following interviews, held with some of the ex-factory women, and told in their own words, give a sense of realism and honesty to these emotions and make an invaluable and essential contribution to the understanding of the character and uniqueness of the Derry factory girl.

Mary Harrigan

The memories of Mary Harrigan (née Donaghey) demonstrate a sense of family loyalty and responsibility that were characteristics of the shirt women:

> On a cold day in January 1951, I walked on my own down Beechwood Street to begin my first day's work in the shirt industry. I was just turned 14 and still wearing white ankle socks as I climbed

The City Factory, Queen Street.

Iconic image of the Derry shirt industry. Star Factory, Foyle Street, circa 1930s.

the concrete stairs of the City Factory. I glanced at the painted brick walls and the cold curved iron handrail, the place looked really daunting. It was a far cry from my wee comfortable school, I thought to myself. Being the oldest girl in our family, I knew my time had come when I was expected to bring some badly needed money into our house in Dawros Gardens. I went to the office and was then taken to the clipping room, where my duties were to be that of a message girl, popularly called the 'gofer' girl and 'get me' girl on the floor, collecting different things from different parts of the factory and bringing them to the girls at their machines. My weekly wages were 18s (90p). Of course, those were the days when you never heard of women going out drinking; how times have changed!

We had sing-alongs daily and we used to listen to the wireless and programmes such as *Music While You Work* and *Housewives' Choice*. It wasn't easy work, but we were all in the same boat so we just got on with it and tried to earn as much money as we possibly could, because, believe me, money was in short supply in those days. I recall we had to do over 21 dozen shirts before our bonus

Bridget Diver hard at work.

would begin. But once you got your tally out of the way, things looked and felt better because we were now earning money over and above our normal weekly wage. Going home on a Friday night with a good bonus was a great feeling, not least because it was hard for men to get good jobs in Derry at that time – a fact which was never far away from our minds, as most family homes suffered from this scourge. We were careful with the little money we had. It was the done thing for three of us girls to get a plate of chips and three forks in Harley's fish-and-chip shop, where Lexi Feeney and Dickie Gallagher would be serving.

I left that City Factory in 1957 to get married, and before I left, like everyone else who was about to be married, I was placed on a trolley and had my hair tied in ribbons and wheeled around the factory floor.

I was married at eight o'clock Mass and the girls all came to the church to see me walking up the aisle. If by some magic wand I could be given the opportunity to go back to the shirt factory, would I go? Yes, in a heartbeat!

Mary White

Mary White (née Doherty) remembers the day she left school as if it were yesterday:

I was so excited when the school bell sounded for the very last time for me on that Friday afternoon way back in 1960. It was time to join the real world, I thought to myself, as I walked the short distance from St Mary's School to our home in Central Drive.

'No more school books, nor no more homework for me,' I said to my mother, rubbing my hands with delight.

My mother stopped what she was doing and looked me straight in the eyes; what she said to me has stayed with me to this very day. 'Mary, daughter, one day you will look back on your school days with nothing but fondness, for those are the days even time itself will not erase from your memory. Monday morning will see the start of you growing up in a world that one day builds you up and the next day kicks you down.'

Still, that Sunday night I couldn't sleep a wink as I was all up to high doh thinking about starting work as a dispatch girl in Hogg and Mitchell's the next morning.

Hogg and Mitchell's,
Little James Street.

I got up at 6.30am and was out the door at 7.15, as I wanted to be early on my first day. The first morning went well and I went home for my dinner at 12.30 and remember telling my mother and older brother Charlie how great the job was. Soon I got my first wage packet of £1-19s which I handed to my mother with pride, mainly because I was the eldest girl in our family, so the first to start work and contribute to the family budget.

Although I liked the job, I wasn't fully content, as I wanted to sew. I'd been sewing at home since my father bought me a sewing machine when I was 14 years old. I loved sewing. So, reluctantly, I left Hogg and Mitchell's and went to work in the Rosemount Factory, where I started as a sewing machinist. My wages rose to £2-2s-6d. I was happy as Larry and the girls were brilliant craic. Actually, it was while I was working there that Olive Quigley took me to my first big dance, which was in the Flamingo Ballroom in Ballymena. I remember it was around Christmas time and her brother's band – Johnny Quigley All Stars – were playing at the dance. I felt all grown-up as I got ready for that, my very first dance.

After two years, I left the Rosemount Factory, the reason being that time-and-motion studies had been introduced and I had heard

the girls in Welch Margetson's were earning really big money doing piecework, so I got a job there. Welch Margetson's was a factory which was mixed with Protestant and Catholic workers, and I must say we all got on well together. By this time, I was really fast at operating the sewing machine and I was dumbfounded, but delighted, when I received my first wage packet on piecework – it was a whopping £12! I must give credit to Margaret Glass, for she was the one who taught me how to increase my speed on the sewing machine. At that time, I still handed my wage packet to my mother, who in turn gave me £2 pocket money, plus my union money. In those days it was very important to keep paying your union dues, and the pocket money my mother gave me was very good, considering it was only 2s-6d to get into Borderland (dance hall).

I stayed in Welch Margetson's even after I married Jim White from the Lecky Road, and, even when I had my first child, I still went back to the factory afterwards. I only left the factory after my second child was born, but I did return for a four-year spell later in Scott's Factory in Patrick Street, finally leaving factory work for good in 1980.

I would have to say I loved life in the shirt factories and the craic and banter was something else, and lifelong friends I made there I could never forget them.

Irene McCarron

Some girls couldn't get leaving school quickly enough to get into the factories. Irene McCarron (née McCallion) was one of them and freely admits that, while most girls started work at the age of 14, she actually started her working life a couple of months before that:

I remember I had to report to the office in Hogg and Mitchell's and after the office workers had a brief discussion between themselves I was taken to the smoothing room and assigned to be a message girl. But soon I progressed to the machines and I was thrilled at that, as now I was one of the fully fledged big girls.

When I let my mind slip back, which I often do, to those beautiful, carefree days of my youth, my first thoughts are of me

Above: A factory laundry department in the 1930s. Below: A 1970s' version.

and my friend Stella Roddy, arms linked, walking to work from our homes in Wellington Street. Although shirt-factory work was hard, we never missed a day, simply because our money was badly needed at home. We never had the luxury of taking a day off, even when you felt a little ill or had a bad cold; you just got up at the usual time and walked to work as normal. My wage packet contained the princely sum of £2-15s-6d, which was duly handed, unopened, to my mother each Friday night. She would hand me back a few shillings for the dance or pictures. Of course, my clothes were bought and paid for each week, as were my union dues. Can you see a young girl today handing her mother a wage packet unopened each week?

Hogg and Mitchell's was my favourite workplace. The girls were the salt of the earth and the men who worked there – in particular, Billy Parkhill, Richard Tollstone and my old floor manager, Mr Caldwell – were gentlemen. They would tap on the 'parlour' door (the toilet) and gently say: 'Time up' if some of the girls were in for a wee smoke and maybe taking too long. Although the floor managers didn't interact much with the girls, they were held in high esteem by most of them. Like a lot of other girls, I moved to other factories in search of better money and I eventually left the factory in 1972 to raise a family.

Mary McCallion

Mary McCallion's sense of family loyalty and responsibility required her to become something of a migrant worker; she became a Derry shirt-factory girl in 1939:

Back in the summer of 1939, I was 14 years old and had just left school and was living with my parents at our wee farm at Quigley's Point, which my father worked on his own. So, of course, it would not be possible to generate enough money from it to raise a family. It was while sitting around a turf fire in our cottage one Sunday night that I, along with my parents, decided the only course of action for me was to go to Derry in search of employment. It was with some excitement and a strange feeling in my stomach that I boarded the bus the following Monday morning for Derry. I was very lucky: I

Neely & Wilkinson Ltd, Strand Road.

got a job as a shop assistant in O'Donnell's shop at Clooney Terrace in the Waterside that very first day, and I was to start the next day. I went home to Quigley's Point, feeling very grown-up and contented. The job seemed to be perfect for me, as it provided lodgings. As I approached our wee cottage, my mother was standing at the door, waiting for me. She was delighted when I told her I was starting work the next day and that the job included board.

Leaving Quigley's Point the next morning, I had that same strange feeling in my stomach. To a young girl it felt like I was going to a completely different world. And I suppose it was, to a degree, as I was going from a small country village in Donegal with a distinct country environment to a big city. It was a definite culture shock for a young country girl. I duly started behind the shop counter that Tuesday morning way back in the summer of 1939. I was happy there and I was paid 3s-6d (17p in today's money) a week, plus board and food. At that time, the shirt factories were busy and looking for workers and paying good money, so, on my next day off, I went over to Wilkinson's Factory to look for a job and got a start as a trainee cuffer. I knew how cuffs were made, for the woman who lived beside me in Quigley's Point was an 'outworker', making cuffs for Byrne's Factory in Ture, and I used to watch her as she worked. I went back to my boss and told him I was leaving after working three months for him and in fairness he wished me well. I stayed in Wilkinson's for a short time, then my friend got me a job in the City Factory and I started on the 'speed belt', making cuffs, I later became a collar bander and finally an examiner.

My first 12 years in the City Factory were happy, although the work was very hard. The conditions were good and it was a clean and airy place. However, in 1952 I was admitted to St Columb's Hospital when I was diagnosed with tuberculosis (TB). I was in hospital for two years and on being discharged I got my old job back a few days later. It was a good job that I decided to come to Derry in 1939 because in 1940 the British Government introduced new working laws which meant if you lived in the Republic of Ireland you were classed as a foreigner, so you needed a work permit to work in the north of Ireland. At that particular time, it was very difficult to get a work permit, as jobs in the North were scarce and some girls who came from Donegal would work as maids in Derry for the better-off people but were only paid £1 a month with full board. So, working in a shirt factory was the best option back then.

Hugh Williamson, production manager of the City Factory, congratulating Mary McCallion and presenting her with a suite of furniture on behalf of the directors of the company on her retirement after almost 44 years. Also present: Joseph McLucas, accountant, and Tess Houston, who presented Mary with a bouquet.

Clare Bridge

For Clare Bridge, that first day working was also something of an integration experience for her:

On a Friday morning in the spring of 1960, I sat on my seat in the bus to St Mary's School in Creggan for the last time and had a great sense of freedom. This was the day I yearned for all my school days, the day I would leave school. However, my feeling of freedom was short-lived, as I started work the following Monday behind a machine, learning the cuffing trade in the City Factory.

It was my very first experience of mixing with Protestant girls, and they soon introduced me to the Mem (Memorial dance hall) a traditionally Protestant venue. I met some of my lifelong friends while working in the shirt factories, people like Isobel Doherty, Margaret Boyle, Mary Clifford and Vera Sheerin. We all lived for the weekends. They coaxed me to go to the big dance halls like the Corinthian and taught me the 'Corinthian crawl', where a couple, locked in a tight, closed-eyes, breath-restricting embrace, shuffled along, 123,123, causing traffic problems on the dance floor.

To be very honest, I was probably the slowest worker in the factory, as I just couldn't seem to get the speed and quality required. The repetitive machine work just didn't suit me, so my

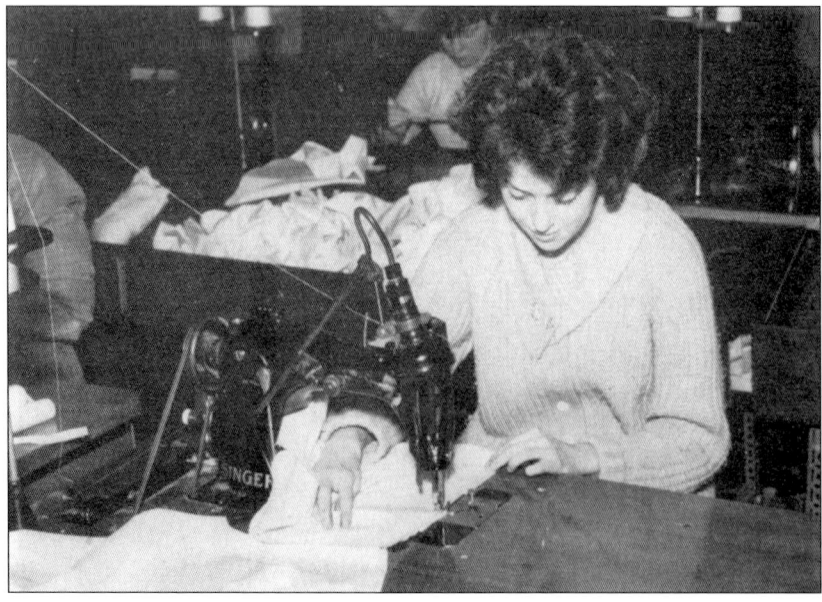

wage was probably one of the lowest in the factory. But I didn't care as long as I got enough to hand in a few pound to the house and had enough left for the weekend dances. Monday morning was hell, as dragging myself out of bed on a cold winter's morning and running down to try to get in before the factory door closed at eight was no joke. However, once I got in to the factory, laughter would soon flow, as that was the morning we all swapped stories about our weekend antics.

I remember Angela, who worked in the corner of the factory floor doing button holes; she was lightning fast, and when she talked, she still kept on working at speed. She was our agony aunt, always listening to our woes and tales of our fall-outs with friends and boyfriends. She certainly got an earful of stories every Monday morning. Her advice was always honest and normally sound.

The first seven years flew in and I left the factory to get married.

To this day, I still have dreams of my time on the factory floor and in those dreams I can still hear the din from the machines and the laughter of the women and girls.

The Memorial Hall (The Mem), Society Street.

Working Together and Wee Buns

All of the city's shirt factories had an integrated workforce; some had a predominantly Unionist workforce, others a predominantly Nationalist workforce, neither imposing their culture on the other except on special annual celebrations when some emblems would appear. Apart from some harmless banter on those special days, the girls worked harmoniously together. On one occasion in Tillie and Henderson, a particular girl, known to be a supporter of the Orange Order, was persuaded that she was required at the top of the collar room, and when she left her machine, the Nationalist girls removed her stool. Returning, she had to stand, which was the plan of deception, whereupon the guilty girls began singing *The Soldiers' Song*, with Kathleen Hone leading the banter: 'There now, Sandra, didn't we say that one day you would stand for our national anthem?' Sandra was quick to reply: 'Is that what they call that tune?' Indeed, it was known that some Catholic girls helped some of the slower Protestant workers to clear up their work so as they

Collar worker Kathleen Hone.

Collar work stops for a photo. Standing, from left: Lily Gurley, Kathleen McCart (supervisor) and Celine McConomy. Seated: Letta Gormley.

could nip out to see the parades, such was the companionship of the factory girls.

There was no formal training at the time for becoming a machinist. What happened was the forewoman would ask a machinist if the young girl could sit beside and watch her working. Being more or less 'family factories', the clippie was placed beside a relative where possible and when the machinist would go on her break, the young girl would have a small piece of cloth and would try working the machine; that's how Mary Harrigan became a machinist in the City Factory:

> After a couple of weeks, I was sat down at a machine for about ten minutes a day and a woman would show me how to operate it. I was keen to get away from being a message girl, so I learnt fast. And soon I was operating a banding machine all day long on my own and earning more money into the bargain.

It could be said that the Derry factory girls were spoiled for choice as to which factory to work in, for although the manufacturing process was identical in all the factories, the various bonus schemes made some factories more attractive than others. Some shirt-factory women were happier in the smaller and more intimate family-owned shirt factories,

Rosemount Factory, Rosemount Avenue.

AE McCandless & Co, Bishop Street.

Star Factory, Foyle Road.

James Hamilton & Co,
John Street.

which could offer more flexible working hours than bonuses. Time for working mothers was as important as the bonus schemes; for them it was the factory floor and the kitchen floor that were intertwined as they combined both to keep the home functioning. For these reasons, there was always movement between factories as some women would seek the most suitable factory to work in.

Between the 1940s and the 1960s, there were upwards of 38 large- and medium-sized shirt factories and a dozen or so small Derry family-owned factories producing shirts in the city (see opposite).

Getting their 'amounts' done, either keeping up with the speed belt or on the 'line' formation, was what made the working day good, bad or indifferent for the individual girl, but all had the realisation of the importance that their earnings brought to the home.

Material piled high as the girls worked hard.

On the speed belt, the speedier girls, having accumulated some 'spare time', became very resourceful and would do some home clothing alterations: some workers were more enterprising and would make patchwork quilts; others would help the slower workers. Some slow workers would pull the passing garment off the belt and work unpaid overtime to 'catch up', such as Eithne Duffy: 'I remember being piled up one day and I ran home for my dinner and ran back again to be in half an hour before the time to get the work done.' Some mammies

FACTORY	ADDRESS	CURRENT USE
AE McCandless & Co	Bishop Street	Commercial
Ben Sherman Ltd	Maureen Avenue	Disused
Black Bear Factory	Clarendon Street	Demolished
Castle Factory	Castle Street	Demolished
City Factory	Patrick Street	Arts/commercial
DA Mooney	Foyle Street	Demolished
Ebrington Factory	Ebrington Gdns	Commercial
Edward Tinney	Society Street	Commercial
Fitright Shirts	Distillery Brae	Commercial
G Scott & Co	Patrick Street	Commercial
Glenaden Shirts	Trench Road	Disused
Graham Hunter	Springtown	Functioning
Hogg & Mitchell	Gt James Street	Apartments
Huntright & Co	Magazine Street	Commercial
James Boyd & Co	Market Street	Commercial
James Hamilton & Co	John Street	Commercial
James Sweeney	East Wall	Demolished
Lloyd, Attree & Smith	Gt James Street	Commercial
McIntyre & Hogg	Foyle Street	Demolished
Mitchell's Factory	Gt James Street	Commercial
Neely & Wilkinson Ltd	Strand Road	Apartments
Northern Factory	Carlisle Road	Demolished
Paragon Factory	William Street	Demolished
Peter England	Campsie	Demolished
Robert Sinclair	Abercorn Road	Commercial
Rocola	Bligh's Lane	Demolished
Rosemount Factory	Park Avenue	Commercial
SM Kennedy & Co	Magazine Street	Commercial
Star Factory	Foyle Road	Apartments
Tillie & Henderson	Foyle Road	Demolished
Welch Margetson	Carlisle Road	Commercial
William Burns & Co	Alma Terrace	Demolished
William Scott	Bennett Street	Demolished

List of large- and medium-sized shirt factories that have existed in the city.

It was heads down and full concentration when times were busy.

and grannies would also hurry home during the extended dinner break, which was generally one and a half hours, to catch up with some housework.

Other options for catch up were more desperate, devious and dangerous as was the mysterious disappearance of the shuttle from the machine (the container of thread underneath the machine and known as the 'under thread'). This effectively immobilised the machine, which meant in practice that the worker coming after the girl whose shuttle was lost could have the time taken to find the shuttle to play catch up. The shuttle was inevitably found on the floor, further down the belt where it rolled after it had 'allegedly' fallen off the machine. Some girls had the dangerous technique of being able to stop the belt by putting their foot on part of the wheel, which brought a sombre-faced mechanic, a demented departmental manager and a ten-minute delay, as Kathleen Duffy remembered:

> Bridie Nash used to get behind and there would be a large pile of shirts beside her. Bridie was able to stop the belt somehow with her foot and then a mechanic was sent for to fix the problem.

Both the machine mechanics and the departmental managers had the ability to either make a good day or a not so good day for the factory

Time for a smile at Lloyd, Attree & Smith.

girls, one to a greater degree than the other. The mechanics were more involved with the girls because a troublesome machine made for them a troublesome day. The sewing machine was a girl's best friend – but only if it was working well. And for that reason it was very much in the interest of the machinist not to antagonise the mechanic and keeping very friendly with them was the common approach among the girls. As one woman put it:

> If you were in with them [the mechanics], you were all right, and you had to be in with them. You couldn't fall out with them. They had the upper hand, they called the tune and they could take all day. Sometime they would say: 'This has to be fixed in the mechanic shop.' And they would bring you a spare machine, and the girls didn't like working with a strange machine. You had to get used to it.

At times, and in the absence of a factory nurse, the mechanic had to come to the assistance of any machinist who had her finger caught by the machine needle. Such mishaps went with the job and didn't cause

A crowded mechanics' shop in Tillie's. From left: Seamus McLaughlin, George Molloy, Paul Doherty, Charlie McLaughlin and Terry McLaughlin. Girls include: Maureen Cooper, Alice Walsh, Gladys Fraser, Isobel Breslin and Annie Burke.

much alarm except to the unfortunate girl, who would turn the wheel backwards and painfully withdraw the needle herself. If the needle broke in her finger, a mechanic was called who would remove it using a pair of fine pliers. One machinist had a more frightening experience resulting from a freak accident, recalled by Mary, a service worker in charge of a conveyor belt:

One day, Margaret Feeney, who had lovely blonde hair, was leaning over her machine when her hair got caught and tangled up in the wheel. She was in a terrible state, crying and very frightened. Some girl was quick thinking and turned off the whole belt and we were able to gently cut some of her lovely hair off and free her. But it was a terrible experience for her.

Marie Kelly and friends enjoy their tea break at Lloyd, Attree & Smith.

Managers had less verbal contact with the girls, for their opinions were generally passed on to the supervisors who would relay them to the girls. Nevertheless, shirt-factory managers were known to be silent admirers of the workers. Ronnie Simpson, a former City Factory manager, spoke of his admiration:

Ronnie Simpson.

With male employment in the city at very poor levels, the importance of female workers to many thousands of households in this city can never be overstated. And I must say, they carried that responsibility with dignity, charm and humour in their everyday jobs in the shirt industry. Their work ethic and skilled labour were never once questioned, as they produced the very highest quality of shirts and garments, and always on schedule. One of the most lasting impressions that I have is that of their humour, which never ceased to amaze me. I can still hear the girls singing at their machines.

Together with the dinner break – which varied in the different factories but usually lasted one and a half hours – work stopped for a ten-minute tea break in the mornings and afternoons and there was also a five-minute break every hour. With no factory canteens at the time, everyone had to make their own arrangements for tea. A former supervisor explained:

You had a wee poke of tea and you went down to the boiler room with teapots, snuff tins with wire handles on them, you name it, and line them all up on the floor for the hot water and you had to be on the ball if you didn't want to wait all morning. For some girls would come along and move their pots to the top of the line; on the way upstairs again, you got scalded.

The tea was always ready and waiting well before the break, along with the buns, ordered and collected by the message girls, from the small shops adjacent to the factories. One such girl in Hogg and Mitchell's explained:

Cheers! From left: Eileen McDaid, Lily Murray, Pat McKeegan and unknown.

Cups at the ready. From left: Margaret O'Kane, Peggy James, Rose O'Kane, unknown and Eilish McLaughlin.

Lizzy Heaney (centre) and friends from Wilkinson's Factory, 1950s.

Above: Lunch break at Maydown: Patsy McIntyre (left) and
Tillie O'Donnell (standing).

Below: Smoke break at Brookhaven Factory with Hazel McCombe on right.

I had to go to Anderson's shop at the bottom of Little Great James Street for buns for the girls. We would get them on 'tick' during the week and pay for them once we got our wages each Friday. That wee arrangement worked well for all concerned, because all the girls would be clean out of money come Monday morning.

Some of the girls preferred to bring bread and have it toasted by the smoothing irons used by the collar smoothers, resulting in the bread being wafer thin, roasting hot and tasty. There was a time when 'bun runs' were not allowed in the factory; no-one was allowed out during working hours, with no exceptions, even for girls working overtime. But the girls were always able to come up with solutions, particularly in Tillie's, where the overtime workers wanted chips with their tea. Bridget Doherty was one of those workers:

We would throw strings out the window on the Foyle Road end of the factory and the girl would tie the parcel of chips from Tracey's for us to pull up. Then one day the manager was looking out the window and saw this parcel rising up past the window, and it didn't take him long to solve the mystery. But he was more amused than annoyed.

Dancing Days and the 'Bars'

The factory girls loved and looked forward to the weekend dances. Mary White spoke of her dancing schedule:

> Friday night we went to Borderland, Saturday we would go to the Corinthian or the Guildhall, and on Sunday we went to the Palindrome in Strabane if we heard there were some fellas we knew that had a car were going and who would give us a lift. If not, it was Borderland again.

The factory girls would go dancing every night if they had the money, which was always scarce, or if they had the negotiating skills of Peggy McCourt and were able to talk their way into the halls. Peggy was friendly with the owner of the very popular Ashfield Hall and when cash was tight some nights, she would try the old 'chat' to talk her way in:

> Many a night we hadn't the money for the dance and had to talk to Willie [the owner] into letting us in free for the last hour or so. He usually did, but at times he was harder to get past than the angel at the Gates of Eden.

Anne Harkin (née McDaid) and her friends got good value for their money and devised a plan that got them two dance-hall visits for the price of one. She related it with more than a little satisfaction in her voice:

> We would go to the Corinthian and if the 'bars' weren't in we would get a pass out to come in again. But we would run down to the Guildhall and stand outside and if we knew anyone coming out with a pass, we would tell them that their 'bars' were up in the Corinthian so we swapped passes, and they went to the Corinthian and we went into the Guildhall to have a 'look see' for our 'bars'.

In her account, Anne used a term that is said to have originated in the shirt factories, ie the 'bars'. This has two meanings: either a boyfriend (or some variation of a love interest) or simply the local news (with a hint of gossip). Its origins are uncertain, but some suggest the term stems from when the factory girls would gain attention from the other girls by rattling the iron safety bars that lay underneath their worktops which were there to protect the workers from getting caught up in the various drive shafts that powered some of the machinery on the speed belt.

Getting 'dolled-up' for the dances and the dates was a cost too much for some girls, who also showed initiative and became make-up artists with do-it-yourself home-cosmetics kits to cut expenses. Anne Harkin describes the do-it-yourself kit:

> It took us ages to get ready for the dance. We had no lacquer or mousse in those days so we used a mixture of sugar and water

The navy arrive in town and join in the fun at The Embassy Ballroom. Entertaining at the mike is Harry Harkin with Josie McIntyre on trumpet.

Miss Derry competition in The Embassy, circa 1960s.

brushed into our hair to hold it in place. Nylons were very hard to get so we tanned our legs with a lotion then pencilled a line on them to make it look as if we were wearing stockings. If we wanted our lips to look glossy we would smear glycerine on them and we used to wet soap to stiffen our eyelashes and eyebrows. There were no Avon Ladies around those days so you had to make do with what you had.

Some girls used the tea breaks seated at their machines to prepare for the weekend dances and their dates; eyebrows were plucked and head set with curlers. Some girls went through the pain barrier and got their ears pierced just to wear earrings, described by Ruby who worked in the smaller Leinster Brothers' Factory:

> You pierced the lobe of the ear with a sewing needle, used a double thread with a small knot at the end and pulled the thread through. Then the thread was cut off, lodging the knot in the ear, where it remained for a week. The ear had to be bathed daily with cold tea to keep the knot pliable and easily removed, leaving a small hole for the earring.

The Monday-morning blues were lifted slightly as the weekend tales of the dancing, romancing and heartbreaks were shouted above the noise of the belt for everyone to hear. There were no secrets on the speed belt, though there were plenty of agony aunts to heal the broken hearts. Irene McCarron, working in Hogg and Mitchell's, described the atmosphere:

> Each Monday morning, the 'bars' about the weekend events at the dances would be the big talking point that day. Not a week went by without some girl finishing with her boyfriend. That particular girl would be down in the dumps, so what the rest of the girls did was to gather around her machine and we would all sing: 'Let him go, let him tarry, let him sink or let him swim, for you're going to marry, a far nicer boy than him.' And soon she was smiling again.

Derry dancers in Borderland. At the front
are Dympna Redden, Teresa McKeever,
Jean Norrby and Susan Norrby.

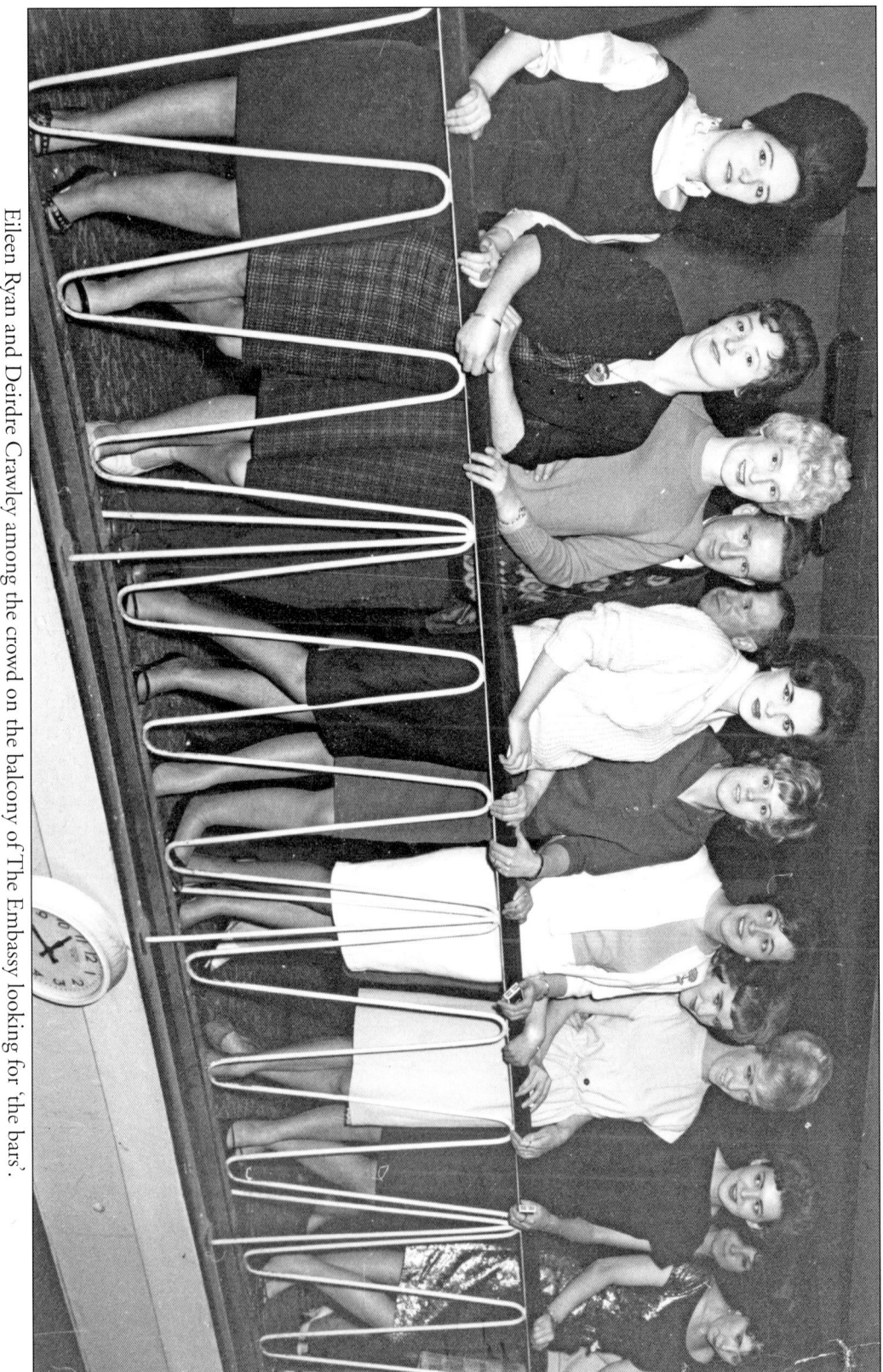

Eileen Ryan and Deirdre Crawley among the crowd on the balcony of The Embassy looking for 'the bars'.

In the Welch Margetson Factory, the weekend heartbreaks were the Monday-morning guessing game on Mary White's line:

God, the craic we had on our line was something else. Never a week went by without someone saying, 'I'm finished with him!' [the boyfriend] and vowing never to speak to him ever again, only to proclaim the next day they were back on again and giving him one more chance. We use to try and guess on a Friday who would fall out with their boyfriends over the weekend; it was a laugh a minute on our line.

Waiting for the results at the Miss Derry competition in The Embassy. Included: John McDermott, Frankie Downey, Arlene McKinney, Susie McFadden and Helen Fitzpatrick.

Not all Monday mornings were good craic, as some girls would have 'wiped the eye' of another at the dances. Peggy McCourt remembers:

At times, some Monday mornings could be slightly awkward, as one of your workmates maybe went with a fellow at the weekend dance that another workmate had just finished with or had their eye on. Oh aye! Some Mondays could be frosty enough on the factory floor, but most of the days the craic was ninety, even though we worked hard and long hours.

At break times the parlours (toilets) would be crowded, particularly on Monday mornings, as they also functioned as a communication and information network where discussions on the weekend 'bars' were not to be missed. Smokers and non-smokers crowded in, though not all had their own cigarettes. Some girls became shareholders in the one cigarette, for the passing-of-the-butt ritual was very popular, as related by Sadie Morris:

You just couldn't afford to buy fags, so the butt was passed between four of us at a time, and if you were the last, you got your lips singed sucking it. And there was always the chat about the sailors. When the ships were in, some sailors would be waiting outside the factory for the girl they had met the last time they were in and the girl would have a head full of curlers ready for the date that night, and then when she saw him, she would go out a different door so he wouldn't see her.

Twist and Shout

Chubby Checker's 1961 international hit *Let's Twist Again* introduced a new era of American dance rhythms such as the Shake, the Jerk, the Watusi, the Locomotion, the Hustle, and Ireland's contribution, the Hucklebuck, the manoeuvres of which were so complicated, dancers simply jived to the music. With these new rhythms, cheek-to-cheek dancing was seen as out of date as couples didn't touch and solo dancing became the norm as couples performed their own body contortions at arm's length from each other. The Twist was an instant hit with the factory girls and became something of a craze. Promoters and entrepreneurs quickly recognised the financial potential of this new fad and Twisting competitions soon became part of the nationwide dance scene. The Derry factory girls were more than able to rise to the challenge of the Twist, having come through the 'Rock Around the

The Star Factory Twisting team go through their routine: Helen Fitzpatrick, Patricia Duffy and Olive Campbell along with their partners Brian Donnelly, John Duffy and Frankie Campbell.

ASTORIA
BUNDORAN

Thursday, 22nd Aug.   9–1. ADM. 5/-.

Mick Delahunty

Friday, 23rd   9–1.30. 7/6.

ALL-IRELAND
TWIST FINAL

Sat. 24th   8–12. ADM. 5/-.   **Sun. 25th**   9–1.30. 6/-.

THE CLEFONAIRES

Mon. 26th, Tuesday, 27th   9–1. 5/-.
Wednesday 28th —   9–1.30. 6/-.

THE HI-LOWS

PHIL O'CONNELL

ALL-IRELAND
TWIST CHAMPIONSHIP
— at the —
ASTORIA BALLROOM
On Friday, 23rd August, 1963
AT 11.30 P.M.

FINALISTS

Mary Regan Ballyshannon, Sean Murray, do.
Maeve Daly, Bundoran, John Wallace, Clifloney.
Nora Miller Ballyshannon, Joe Meehan, Garrison.
Nora Patterson, Enniskillen, Gerry Carty, do.
Phyllis Kane Ballyshannon, Charlie Rooney, do.
Marie Gallagher, Bundoran, Fred Neill, Enniskillen.
Vera Foley, Kinlough, Peter Kelly, Enniskillen.
Brenda Clancy, Limerick, John Marietti, Italy.
Mary Whelan, Moneygold, Andy Conway, Clifloney.

Mary and J. J. Gallagher, Ballyshannon.
Nancy Keenan, Garrison, Kevin McTiernaN, Belcoo.
Gabrielle Leydon Clifloney, John Gilbride do.
Teresa Carty, Garrison, Eileen Nealon, do.
Eliz. Lafly, Ballyshannon, Pat Sheil, do.
Eileen McCann, Moneygold, Liam McHugh, Clifloney.
Mary Farrell, Dublin, J. Coughlan, Ballymara.
Bronté Meily, Dunsleary, Sean Ward, Dunglee.
Joan Dunne, Belfast, Brian McGinn Omagh.

Agnes Doherty, Lifford, Glena Daly, Bundoran.
Teresa Aylward, Dublin, Brian Peesley, Enniskillen.
Ann Gormley, Kesh, Sean Falls, Dungannon.
Carol Meade Bundoran, P. V. Dolan, Bundoran.
Joan and Seamus Granaghan, Bundoran.
Mary Daly, Bundoran, P. Toway, Ballaghaderreen.
Ann Crilly, Omagh, Bren Bartoigan, Collooney.
Mary McConnell, Bellast, F. McDonald, Belturbet.
Esthur Fergin Belfast, Eugene Corrigan, Bawnboy.

WINNING COUPLE RECEIVE NEW 1963 PRINZ 4 N.S.U. MOTOR CAR

CONLANS' SALES
Co. Leitrim — Wardhouse, Tullaghan.
BY PRIVATE TREATY
FOUR-APARTMENT COTTAGE
TOGETHER WITH TWO ACRES OF LAND
situated at Sligo-Bundoran road
Further particulars from Auctioneer or Alfred McMorrow,
12 B. Scillitoe, having carriage of sale.
Bundoran — Leeson House

MEEHAN'S SALES
Ballyshannon, Co. Donegal.
PRELIMINARY NOTICE
IMPORTANT AND ATTRACTIVE SALE OF
RESIDENTIAL BUSINESS PROPERTY
together with Ten Acres Approximately
of Prime Fattening Land.
Situate in the Townland of CARRICKBOY, Ballyshannon

ALL-IRELAND "TWIST" CHAMPIONS WIN CAR

There was wildly enthusiastic applause from a capacity audience in the Astoria Ballroom, Bundoran, on Friday night when Helen Kelly, Derry, and John Crawford, Ballyshannon, were declared winners of the Phil O'Connell All-Ireland Twist Championship. Mr. Crawford was chaired by fans to the bandstand where he and Miss Kelly were presented with the key of the N.S.U. Prinz 4 car, the prize for the competition, by Mr. O'Connell.

The competition aroused tremendous interest throughout Ireland and the finalists were drawn from the four corners of the country. Jim Byrne, a member of the Irish Board of Dancing, had a difficult task adjudicating and eventually reduced the finalists to five couples from whom the eventual winners were selected.

Music was provided by the popular Viscounts.

N.U. TAILORS AND GARMENT WORKERS
(DERRY BRANCH)

SHIRT QUEEN DANCE
will be held in
Derry Guildhall,
WEDNESDAY, MARCH 26,
at 8 p.m.
ADMISSION   2s 6d

DERRY SHIRT QUEEN COMPETITION

FOURTEEN FINALISTS SELECTED

The fourteen finalists in the Londonderry Shirt Queen competition were selected on Thursday by a selection committee, the members of which were Messrs. L. Stuart, P. J. Flanagan, J. H. Ruddock and Commander Geddings, O.B.E., R.N.

The finalists, who will go before the judges next week for final adjudication, are as follows:—

Mrs. Clifford (City Factory), Miss O'Hea (Tillie & Henderson), Miss F. McVeigh (Richards), Miss B. Smyth (Lloyd Attree), Miss E. Norris (Hogg & Mitchell), Miss L. Doherty (Mooneys), Miss B. McCall, Miss P. Gillen, Miss L. McShane (Hogg & Mitchell), Miss M. Deehan (Rosemount), Miss A. O'Connell (Richards), Miss E. Cremond, Miss N. Breslin, Miss S. McDermott (City Factory).

'Clock' and 'Jitterbug' eras of the American sailors. None more so than Helen Kelly, who worked in Hogg and Mitchell's and who won the All-Ireland Twisting Competition held in Bundoran, County Donegal. Helen tells her story:

> We went up to Bundoran for our August holidays, 12 of us, three in a bed, and we went dancing in the Astoria Ballroom, where heats for the All-Ireland Twisting Queen were on. I was out dancing with this fella who asked me to partner with him, so we took part. It was really hard work: there were three heats over three nights. We got through to the final and I just couldn't believe it when we were announced the winners. The prize was a car (NSU Prinz) that we sold for £600, for it would cost a lot of money, which we hadn't got, to take it across the border to Derry. We halved the money and I bought a big new tiled fireplace for the house.

Helen Kelly and partner, winners of the 1962 Phil O'Connell All-Ireland Twisting Championship held in the Astoria Ballroom, Bundoran, pictured with their winning prize, a new car.

Twisting the tide away on Buncrana shore – Margaret Boyle and Clare Bridge.

Amazingly, the following year another Derry factory girl, Olive McGinty, and her boyfriend, Frankie Campbell, won the same competition. They also won a car and had to sell it for the same reason as Helen and they got £400 for it. The new American dancing routines were soon replaced with the rise of the Irish showbands era and cheek-to-cheek dancing made a strong comeback. Weekend dancing for the factory girls was now becoming more expensive, for they now had to travel to the new venues starting up in Donegal at Muff, Buncrana and Letterkenny. Nevertheless, the factory girls left the city in droves at the weekends in a variety of buses to Borderland, the Fiesta and Plaza dance halls. For some girls, travelling to the dances had its advantages, as one remarked: 'If you didn't get a dance with yer fella, you might get a chat with him on the bus home and maybe get off with him.'

Above: Olive McGinty and Frankie Campbell, Twist champions.
Below: Smiling winners of the 1963 All-Ireland Twisting Championship.

Above left: Olive McGinty and Frankie Campbell performing their winning dance in Bundoran.

Above: Olive and Frankie holding their trophies from the semi-finals in Cresslough, County Donegal.

Left: A couple giving a twisting exhibition to onlookers.

Twisting became all the rage in the dance halls.

Factory Queen Dances

Among the most eagerly awaited events was the annual Factory Queen dance, organised by management and Trade Unions, which involved a contest. The first Factory Queen dance took place in the Derry Guildhall in March 1947 when 16 finalists from eight factories competed for the title, which was won by a Philomena Gillen from Hogg and Mitchell's. The popularity and success of that first contest, and the financial potential of such an event, were recognised by local entrepreneurs, and that guaranteed its continued promotion well into the 1990s when it imitated the Rose of Tralee Festival with each contestant having to perform over two nights by singing, dancing or playing a musical instrument. Derry businessman (and co-author) Willie Deery, who promoted several such events, describes the pageantry of the 1994 Factory Queen contest:

> All 13 contestants were transported in a fleet of limousines from the Everglades Hotel into the city, where they paraded down Shipquay Street – led by a pipe band and the outgoing Factory Queen, Patricia O'Kane, resplendent in a pink Cadillac – to the Guildhall. The event was a sell out, so a CCTV broadcast of the proceedings in the Guildhall was 'piped' live into Squires Nightclub, which also had a 'house full' notice posted. The competition was hosted by Paul Clark of UTV and was won by Caroline McDaid, who worked in Desmond's Factory at Drumahoe.

The first Factory Queen, Philomena Gillen.

Philomena Gillen receiving an award from Hugh McDonald, the Donegal film star who appeared in the film *The Seventh Veil*.

The 1947 Derry Shirt Factory Queen, Philomena Grant, crowning the 1979
Queen, Bernadette Cassidy of the City Factory, in the El Greco night club.
The runners up included: Collette Devenney, Christine McCann, Helen
McGinley and Eilish Harkin. Among the event organisers and sponsors are:
Betty Brown, Ann Bryson, Noel McBride, Dessie Coyle and Eddie Davis.

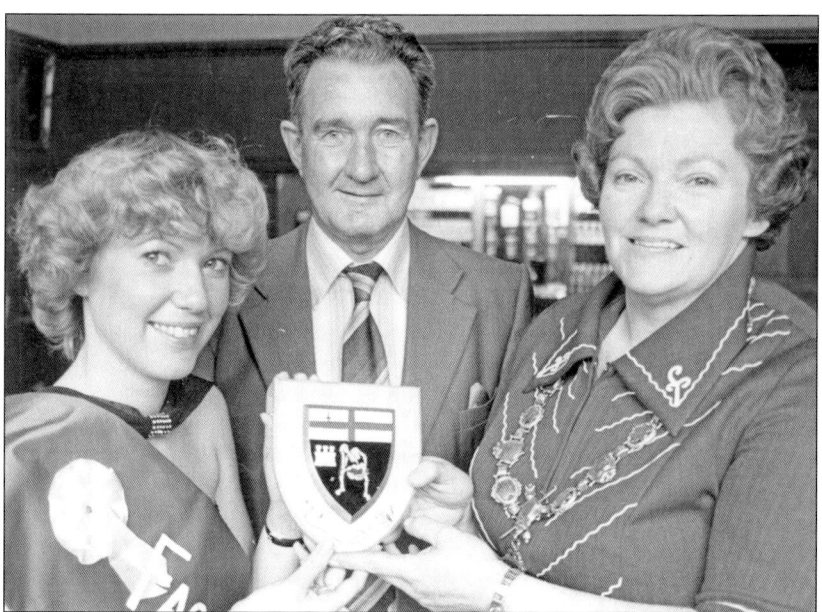

Mayor Marlene Jefferson presents 20-year-old Eilish Harkin with a plaque
of the city's coat of arms after Eilish was crowned Derry Factory Queen for
1980. Joining them in the Mayor's Parlour of the Guildhall is the competition
organiser Eddie Davis.

Factory Queen organiser Eddie Davis presents the contestants in the 1970 competition.

Factory Queen promoter Willie Deery is surrounded by happy contestants during the 1994 competition.

Paul Clarke of UTV with the judging panel and organisers of the 1994 Factory Queen completion won by Caroline McDaid. Included: Michael Doherty, Diane Stevenson, Margaret Stewart, Bernie Mount, Shaun Doherty, Paul Rogers, Charlie Nash, Michael Deery and event promoter Willie Deery.

Paul Clarke chats with the Factory Queen
from Desmond's in Drumahoe.

A contestant representing Fruit of the Loom
serenades the audience.

One of the contestants displays her musical talent with a button accordion.

Audience members cheer as the contestants enter the stage in the final of the
1994 Factory Queen competition.

Audience members celebrate after the winner is announced.

Caroline McDaid, proud 1994 Factory
Queen winner.

Caroline McDaid celebrates her success
with the two runners-up.

Romance and Rituals

Being a naval port at the time, Derry had sailors of all nationalities and also had a permanent contingent of Americans stationed at the Clooney Communications Base in the Waterside. It was a time of Hollywood and the stars for some Derry factory girls – and a walking-home-alone time for the Derry men. For some girls, 'getting off' with a Yank at the Embassy was the spot prize and generally resulted in, according to some parlour talk, a stroll out the Letterkenny Road to the Daisy Field or a 'lark in the Waterside park'. But most factory girls, again according to parlour talk, still preferred the Derry boys.

Some Americans came to the dances, hoping to meet an Irish colleen. Mary Lynch, a front stitcher, recalls a chat in the parlour:

> One time the talk was about Americans from the base and one girl let it slip that one of them wanted to meet a red-haired factory girl with freckles at Littlewoods corner on that next Friday night. About four of us went that night to Littlewoods corner, me with my leg tan and high heels. But he was attracted to a lovely red-haired girl called Margaret Barr. It was only a bit of fun on our part and nothing serious came out of it.

Most of the city's large factories got their share of government shirt orders during the war years and some of the girls took this opportunity to send notes to the forces by slipping a wee note into the pocket of a shirt with their name and address. The note would be short and to the point – 'If you're single, drop us a line; if you're married, never mind' – in the hope that some nice young single American would contact them.

It worked for one City Factory girl, whose experience was put into verse by well-known local musician and author Seamus McConnell:

> I put a letter in the shirt and shipped it off to war,
> A Yank wrote back and said he'd like to meet me in a bar.
> He was six-feet tall and handsome, was brought up in LA,
> And now he wants to marry me and take me far away.

So it's goodbye to the City Factory, goodbye to Creggan Heights,
I'm off to California to see all those bright lights.
I've got my Yank, I'll have six kids and live life in the sun,
My days in the City Factory making shirts are well and truly done.

I said goodbye to all the girls at the Embassy and the Crit,
We married in St Eugene's, my man was quite a hit.
We cruised across the ocean and landed in New York,
Took a train to California to the sunshine and no more work.

And now we live in Fresno, with our six kids and the smog,
I often think of the Creggan, Irish Street, the Fountain and the Bog.
I think of all the factory girls, Carlisle Road, Strand Road and the Foyle,
Nights dancing with sailors and those days of humour and toil.

I was a GI bride once, but now I'm middle class,
I've got no time for bigotry, cause it is such an ass.
Still when I think of Derry and the daily factory grind,
I yearn for all my friends still there and the things I left behind.

(Courtesy: Seamus McConnell)

It was almost impossible for factory girls leaving to get married to slip out unnoticed in order to avoid the traditional, terrifying ritual they had to endure, because it generally was their close friends who tipped off the other workers. The ritual was inclined to get out of hand at times, as Phyllis Moran experienced:

They tied my hair up with ribbons and it took me nearly a couple hours to get them off to go home. Then they started to carry me from the room I worked in and I got very nervous with them for doing this and I battered and thumped them. There was one wee girl near me, I didn't know who she was. She had lovely blonde hair and I grabbed her by the hair and nearly pulled it out of her. It was terrible. You didn't know what they would do next.

Bridie Cooke (née McCloskey) had a less frightening, though a more embarrassing, experience:

I was able to get out of the factory without any fuss because I had left work a few days before and was walking home when the rain came on. I put up my umbrella and was showered with shirt buttons. The girls had stuffed them into my umbrella. The people on the street didn't know what happened and I could do nothing but blush.

Though the ritual was frightening, all was forgotten at 'the big night' when the bride-to-be was given her wedding present from the workers, which was generally a very practical gift. Usually these gifts, according to some of those interviewed, would have been bed linen, a lemonade jug and glasses, pillow sets or a box of cutlery. But most popular were the tea sets, with some girls claiming to have got as many as three and four. The actual wedding-day festivities were not too long-drawn out, as Berna McDermott recalls:

The thing that amazed me in those days was that a girl was able to get married, have her photo taken, be at the reception and still catch the three o'clock train at the GNR station for Dublin. Then, as the train sounded the whistle and slowly passed Tillie's, all the girls would hang out the windows on the Foyle Road side, waving and shouting.

Going to Dublin for their honeymoon was popular at the time and it was seen as an exciting, and unusual, trip away for most Derry people who normally could not afford staying at a hotel there for any extended length of time. As Stella McDaid put it: 'Dublin was another world – Buncrana was as far as most people got to.'

Helping Hands

The more immediate material and social needs of the girls were supplied through the unique shirt-factory culture of lotteries and clubs. The lotteries gave access to a lump sum of money and a lottery draw could be organised by anyone in the factory provided they could recruit a reliable number of girls to pay a certain amount of money over a certain number of weeks for an agreed amount of payout money. Lotteries could be extended over five, ten, 15 or 20 weeks, with payouts varying from £5 to £20, depending on the popular demand.

There were various reasons for women starting a lottery, as Margaret Nelis, a front stitcher, explains: 'It might be a personal emergency, like covering First Communion expenses.' Maisie McLaughlin gave a more practical reason: 'It was a good way of getting a rise.'

Through the various clubs, clothes, shoes, photographs, bedding and household goods all could be got and strictly controlled by the 'pay-up-on-Friday' code. The club agent for the various city shops would go guarantor and give a signed note for a certain amount of money to the particular person to take to the particular shop.

The photo clubs were very popular, primarily because cameras were a luxury item. Several girls would share the cost of the club, as Eithne Duffy recalls: 'Theresa McMonagle and I took the club between us. It was about a shilling (5p) each a week for, I think, 20 weeks.'

Friday afternoon in the factories was like a money-exchange market as debts were paid and collections made. The different lottery and club organisers could be seen moving frantically through the machine rooms, looking for and collecting from their clients. Others could be seen collecting for churches and charities, rattling their empty snuff tins and waving empty cardboard button boxes at everybody. The 'giving culture' had a strong tradition among the Derry factory girls, who had an ongoing relationship with the charitable and voluntary organisations within the city. Maisie McLaughlin remembers:

We always collected for the Nazareth House and sent the wanes selection boxes at Christmas and chocolate eggs at Easter and some girls would bring in real eggs instead of the chocolate ones.

Happy Days and Annual Outings

Factory management and Trade Unions alike were also anxious to foster good working relationships and keep the girls happy and content at their work. Factory canteens were introduced, music was piped into the factories from the BBC's *Workers Playtime* radio programme through Tannoy sound systems. Music by choice was then introduced with the installation of the radio-record player in the mechanics' workroom that gave the girls an option to have their favourite record played and gave the mechanics a headache as they became part-time DJs being always pestered by the girls to play their favourite song.

In Tillie and Henderson, a more bizarre idea to keep the workers happy was introduced by management, who painted all the machines green on the recommendation of industrial psychologists, popular at the time with factory managers, who suggested that certain colours had a tranquilising effect and brought contentment. To the Monday-morning workers, it brought shock and the feeling that someone in management required hospital treatment.

All these approaches to foster good working relationships were supported by various other social activities that included bus outings

A Tillie's outing in the 1940s.

to Donegal, shopping trips to Belfast, and train excursions to Portrush. The Christmas and New Year dances were not-to-be-missed events, as was the annual factory dinner dance, which was generally a two-part affair with management, staff and selected supervisors 'at table', and afterwards they would join the dancers. For some girls, a dance with the manager just made their night, but they would regret it in the parlour the next morning.

Tillie's football supporters. Three laundry workers in Belfast for a Derry City match: Kathleen Smith, May Parkhill and Hanna Devlin.

Star Factory workers going on a train excursion in the 1940s. Included: Kathleen McCafferty, Lily McCafferty, Lily Lynch, John Lynch and James Toland.

Soaking up the sun on an outing.

A Gullen Mitchell Factory bus outing to the Glens of Antrim and Portrush.
Workers gather around the manager, Mr B Mitchell (centre). Included: Teresa
McGilloway, Annie McGinley, Mary Campbell, Alban Norrby, Sally O'Kane,
Margaret McCourt, Jack McCarron and wife, and Agnes O'Neill.

A Richies Factory outing to the beach.

Fun at Portrush. Back seat: Breidge Carlin and unknown. Middle: Kathleen
McFeely and unknown. Front: Mary Carlin and Mona Kivelehan.

Three Tillie's ladies at Portrush.
Joanna Dean, Molly Martin and Eithne Duffy.

A McCandless Factory outing in the 1960s.

Picnic at Grianan. Standing: Eileen Sharkey. Sitting, from left: Kathleen Breen, Peggy Murray, unknown, May Parkhill and Sadie Doherty. At front: Frances Harkin.

Factory girls on a religious outing.

Richies Factory staff on a bus outing, 1940s.

Frolics on the beach during a City Factory bus run. Included: Nell Doherty, Margaret Lynch, May Lynch, Ann McDaid and Evelyn Doherty.

A City Factory bus run. Back, from left: Eileen Nicholl, Evelyn Doherty, Nell Doherty and May Lynch. Front: Margaret Lynch and Anne Harkin.

Changing Times

The swinging sixties marked a dividing line in the story of the Derry factory girl. Changes were taking place on the factory floor that gave the girls a bit of a culture shock. The traditional speed belt and 'line' methods of production of over 100 years' standing disappeared, both replaced with the introduction of new Time Study Engineering (TSE) production methods.

The introduction of TSE, known as 'time study', dramatically changed the working practices on the factory floor. The Derry factory girl was soon to discover that the clock moved faster than the speed belt and the working day was now to be measured in minutes rather than hours. It was the larger factories that introduced time study; the smaller and family-owned factories continued to operate their own various incentives and working conditions.

Basically, under time-study working, each girl was responsible for her own earnings. With the incentive to earn more, the faster the girl worked, the more she earned; the slower she worked, the less she earned. This was in contrast with the old system where every girl had the same money for doing the same required set amount. Each 'bundle' of work the girls completed now had a time limit in terms of minutes attached on a work ticket, and the girls' total weekly minutes determined how much they got in their pay packet at the end of the week ie the more minutes, the more money. Some slower workers would play the 'dead horses' race with the tickets, which meant they would put in tickets for work they had not completed and then it was back to the old game of playing 'catch up'. Speedier machinists would withhold tickets from work that they had completed and would keep them as a reserve should a 'rainy day' come in a week when they would have the more difficult new-fashion nylon shirts to stitch. This manipulation of the work tickets reflected the difference between the mixed ability of the workers, as one woman explained:

> None of us were the same, so how could the time-study engineers say that all the side seamers were able to do this amount and all the front stitchers could do that amount? Maybe two or three could do it, but there were another ten or so who couldn't. They set the

amounts for what they wanted; all they wanted was for one girl to do the amounts, then they would argue everyone should do them.

This new system changed the whole working atmosphere within the factories, affecting working relationships and creating controversy and competition among the girls to chase the extra money as some tried to make sure they got the big bundles of work so as to avoid constantly changing the different-colour thread as was the case with the smaller bundles. For the speedier workers, the introduction of time study meant good money could be earned and they earned it while most of the slower workers settled for the guaranteed basic minimum wage. Chatting and smoking in the parlours was now costing time and money. The singing, sewing girls on the speed belts and on the 'line' gradually became the competitive, isolated and captive workers of TSE as they were corralled in their own work space and the singing, which had been infectious on the belt, was greatly reduced.

For some of the factory girls, TSE brought bad times:

It was nerve-wracking. The time-study man would tell you just to work as normal and steady, and you just sat and went round the work at your normal speed, but then they would turn round and say to you: 'I know you can go quicker than that.'

We were killed for our money, we didn't get the money for what we put out; it was very unfair. You hadn't time to bless yourself never mind sing.

The speed belt used to be a holiday camp, for no matter what happened, your wages were steady. If you didn't work hard, you had little wages with the time and motion.

Tickets were just your life. They meant everything to you, and then when you counted them at the end of each day, you would say to yourself, 'Dear God, I thought I had more than that.'

It was a bit of an affliction, all diving about getting their amounts. Time study worked on the girls' fear.

Memories of Tillie's by Patrick Durnin

Researching for this publication and interviewing the ex-factory shirt girls reminded me of my own working life in Tillie and Henderson's, which gave me great satisfaction, and I would like to share it here.

On Monday 3 September 1950, I climbed up the iron steps of the Tillie and Henderson shirt factory as a very apprehensive, shy, nervous and a little excited youth of 15 years to begin my working life as an apprentice shirt cutter. Events happened so quickly that I couldn't quite believe what was happening. I had been at school the Saturday before, then afterwards went to watch Derry play in the Brandywell with my father who told me at half time I would be starting work the following Monday. I left school reluctantly because I was starting to like it, as I was being taught Irish and French.

I started my apprenticeship doing 're-cuts', which in practice meant I was to replace any damaged collars or cuffs that the girls would bring – and they brought plenty – though I was told it was an excuse to see the 'wee new boy in the cutting room'. My immediate supervisor wasn't too pleased at several girls standing with me and thought I was chatting them up, when in fact they were trying to get a particular girl 'fixed up' with me. I was beginning to like my job, especially when I gave my mother my first pay.

In Tillie's, as it was affectionately known, I was soon to learn all the attributes that were thought to make one an adult: smoking, gambling, borrowing, learning to dance and noticing girls, which went with the job. It was noticing a particular girl that almost cost me my job after only about six months. This particular girl came to me for a re-cut and had an abundance of white powder on her face. When I asked her jokingly if someone had hit her with a flour bag, it brought the immediate response of tears and a later embarrassing reprimand for me from her supervisor. An equally embarrassing incident happened at another time when the factory manager doing a 'walkabout' in the cutting room came across some bundles of cut collars placed on the floor awaiting removal to the collar room. He made a remark to me which I did not hear, so in my best manners I said 'pardon' to which he replied 'pardon me f***'. I knew then I was in the real world of work.

A more embarrassing incident happened not long afterwards when I decided to venture a walk through one of the machine rooms to view the 'talent'. On that particular day I was wearing a pair of bright yellow socks which was noticed by some of the girls and on my return journey I got the 'rattle', which involved the girls hammering their scissors against their machines, which left me with a very bright red face. I didn't do that again for a long time afterwards.

It was in the factory that I learned to dance as a matter of urgency, as some girls were reporting that I was something of a wallflower at the dances. And so, with the help of the late Willie 'Duke' Doran, dance lessons took place in the cutting room during tea break. Willie handed me a two-handled bin used for the rags and told me to put my arms around it while he started counting:

Traditional cutting room.

One, two, three, one, two, three, and at the same time whistling *The Cuckoo Waltz*. Unfortunately, the swinging sixties put an end to old-time waltzing and I was back on the wall again.

The dispatch area became something of a social club during the lunch break, with activities including darts matches, general knowledge contests and card schools, and was but one of what could be called 'women-free zones'. The other such zones were the carpenters' and painters' workshops, the boiler room and the stockroom. Hospitality was always assured in the boiler room, with its constant supply of hot water for making a cup of tea or a wash and shave if one was late getting into work. The carpenters' shop resembled a conference centre at times, with cutters, mechanics, carpenters and painters all debating and discussing world and local affairs, for at that time, during the 1950s and '60s, there were approximately 33 men and five apprentices employed in Tillie's.

Like all shirt factories, Tillie's had its own indoor market, where anything and everything could be had 'on tick' (credit) until Friday and unfortunately my spending knew no limits: sweets, cigarettes, buns, home-made apple tarts and a loan of money. One woman had a vibrant trade in smuggled cigarettes from across the border and so I became a smoker of Sweet Afton. I soon stopped buying the apple tarts when I found traces of snuff among the icing sugar on the top, as the particular woman who sold them liked to snuff.

With a loan of money from one of the more affluent cutting-room staff, Charlie Cauley, I was able to tell the girls who would appear at my re-cut table with their head covered in curlers that I would be at Borderland that night to see the Clipper Carlton. By that time, I had learned to dance cheek-to-cheek and was now a fully trained band-knife man (large circular rotating knife) with two cut fingers and a cut thumb on my left hand to prove it. Sometimes the more enterprising girls came looking for pieces of cloth and waste cuttings to supply their various activities making patchwork quilts, men's handkerchiefs, children's undergarments, street buntings and flags. I always bartered with them as to how many of my own cut shirts they would 'make up' for me, one of the perks of the trade.

When news of my intending marriage got leaked I had the run of my life. Three girls chased after me with the intention of putting me through the traditional ritual of being bound hand and foot, put in a trolley basket and paraded through the factory. They chased after me along Foyle Road and down the quay and at the Guildhall they were still running after me shouting and screaming, much to the amusement of onlookers. I eventually reached home and fell asleep with exhaustion on the sofa.

Eventually, some 22 years later in September 1972, I walked down Tillie and Henderson's steps for the last time, but now as a redundant shirt cutter. By then it was a radically different factory floor from the one I first worked on, and for me the factory horn sounded no more.

Tillie and Henderson's transfer to Maydown

REDUNDANCY FIGURE CUT AFTER TALKS

MINISTRY'S ASSURANCES TO UNION REPRESENTATIVES

The number of workers who will be redundant when Messrs. Tillie & Hendersons Ltd. transfer their shirt-making operations from their existing factory at Foyle Road, Derry, is 84. The original estimate was 200.

And the Ministry of Commerce has given an assurance that if the operation at Maydown proves viable it will be prepared to erect a new factory for the firm, on the west side of the Foyle.

This news came following talks between representatives of three unions – the Irish Transport and General Workers, the National Union of Tailors and Garment Workers and the Amalgamated Transport and General Workers Union – directors of the firm and officials of the Ministry of Commerce in Belfast.

In a statement issued yesterday on behalf of the union representatives it was stated that they had expressed grave misgivings about the proposed transfer of the company's plant to Maydown and indicated the serious social problems which would arise from any substantial movement of industry from the west bank.

After further discussion a specific assurance was given by the Ministry that if the operation of Tillie and Henderson's was proven viable at Maydown, the Ministry would be prepared to erect a suitable factory for the firm on the west side of the river. Furthermore, the Ministry indicated that they would erect immediately a pre-fabricated building alongside the new premises, to accommodate a cutting room. As a result of that decision the number of workers to become redundant will be reduced from 200 to 84.

The unions firmly impressed on the Ministry that if the company operation at Maydown was successful the unions would expect the Ministry to honour the undertaking to provide a new factory, and that they would again approach the Ministry on the matter in six months' time.

OLD DERRY SHIRT CONCERN WILL CLOSE TODAY

Tillie and Henderson's shirt factory at the Maydown industrial estate, near Derry will close down today. Its closure will end a 130-year link with the city.

The company, which previously had premises at the city end of Craigavon Bridge, employed over 1,000 people, but in recent years it has suffered the same economic setbacks as other textile manufacturing factories and in November, 1972, it closed its factory in the city and moved to Maydown.

Derry received a shock in December last when the company announced that 240 of the 290 workers there would lose their jobs. Despite efforts by the I.T. & G.W.U., these lay-offs took place.

The company's factory in the Co. Donegal town of Carndonagh has also experienced difficulties and seven weeks ago it was announced that it would be closing down.

So far 85 of the 190 work force there have been paid off but the Carndonagh Industrial Action Committee, formed in an attempt to save the Carndonagh operation, has being trying to form a private company.

The official receiver is in Carndonagh and is at present trying to sell the factory there as a going concern.

No date has been set for the closure of the factory but if efforts by the Industrial Action Committee are unsuccessful a date between the end of May and the middle of June is likely.

A Fitting Tribute

A final reminiscence from Mary McCallion would be a fitting tribute to the amazing story of Derry's shirt-factory women and young girls. As noted earlier, Mary came from Quigley's Point into Derry in 1939 aged 14 and found work in the City Factory:

> Those were tough times in Derry for women and girls, as the burden of keeping the wolf away from the door rested mainly with them. Looking back, though, there was a lot of laughter in the air in the shirt factories, maybe because we were all in the same boat and leaned on each other in many ways. So I believe we provided comfort to each other in times of need, and if truth be told, in some cases, despair. Without the shirt factories, and the work they provided for the local women and girls, surviving in Derry would have been very difficult indeed. The employment they provided back then meant that the family unit could be kept together in their home town. Without them, the only alternative would have been the emigration boat for many families. I eventually retired from the City Factory in 1984 after working there 44 years. I got a long-service award and was presented with a lovely three-piece suite of furniture. The passage of time can take away your youth, and even your good looks, but the memories remain. And I have many wonderful memories of the City Factory. Would I change anything about my working life? No, not one minute of it. I worked hard, but the memories of all the lovely women and girls I met and worked with in the factory will live in my heart forever.

With the ending of the swinging sixties, the changing social, political and economic conditions brought a major cultural shock to the city. The shirt factories were closing against foreign competition, political and sectarian unrest on the streets effectively ended the showband craze, and the city entered a much different social era far removed from the factory floor and dance-floor era of the Derry factory girl.

Above and below: Factory women in a sit down protest in Waterloo Place
after several co-workers had been arrested, 1969.

Factory workers in the Bogside, protesting about the arrest of MPs in 1969.

Factory workers marching in protest.

Factory girls amongst anti-internment protesters,
marching down Shipquay Street in 1974.

The anti-internment protesters reach Guildhall Square.

Epilogue

Just as today, large sections of the general public and younger generation are unaware of the social history represented by the large shirt-factory buildings around Derry; similarly, the girls who worked in them at the time had no concept of the extent of the industry they were helping to build. Authentic research has shown that the Derry shirt industry at the opening years of the 20th century was the largest industry in the city with 30 factories employing 6,000 women and exporting worldwide at its peak one million units of the famous Derry 'white shirt' that gave rise to the term 'white-collar worker'. Also, statistics from the then Ministry of Commerce revealed that in 1955 a total of 7,250 were employed in the shirt and collar industry in Derry.

The industry lasted for over 150 years with varying degrees of production and employment numbers and was a way of life as much as a way of earning a living. Life on the factory floor resembled that of a close-knit community that provided for the social, emotional and economic needs of the women and young girls. Any personal problems could be discussed in heart-to-heart talks in the smoking parlours, also seen among the girls as communications centres. The factory floor at times was like an indoor market having a business activity based on credit with a strict pay-up-on-Friday code and where anything and everything could be got 'on tick'. The culture of clubs and lotteries ensured goods and services – clothes, shoes, household goods and money – became that bit easier to have, which gave substantial and immediate help to family life, especially in times of emergencies.

For the young, fun-loving factory girl, the work floor and the dance floor were firmly intertwined and for the mothers and grannies, the work floor and kitchen floor were also closely linked. Family loyalty was a strong characteristic among the factory girls and probably came at the cost to some school leavers of abandoning their personal preferences to pursue their education. Stories of working in the shirt factories are permanent episodes of Derry's folk history and I hope this publication can be seen as an appreciation and admiration of the spirit of the women and girls who sewed and sweated, laughed and cried in all Derry's shirt factories. It is also hoped that the campaign

Attending Stormont to lobby for a statue to be erected in Derry to honour the contribution made to the city of the shirt-factory workers over the years are: Maeve McLaughlin MLA with former City Factory girls Clare Bridge, Isobel Doherty and Mary Clifford. At back: Gretta Ewing.

so passionately and tenaciously pursued by some ex-factory women to have a sculpture erected, acknowledging the massive contribution of the Derry factory women and girls to the city, will find enthusiasm within the city Council.

Finally, it makes an interesting thought as to what sort of a city there would be if the factory horns were to be heard once more and the Derry factory girls were to be seen hurrying to their work again to earn their keep and share the 'bars' with friends, relatives and neighbours.

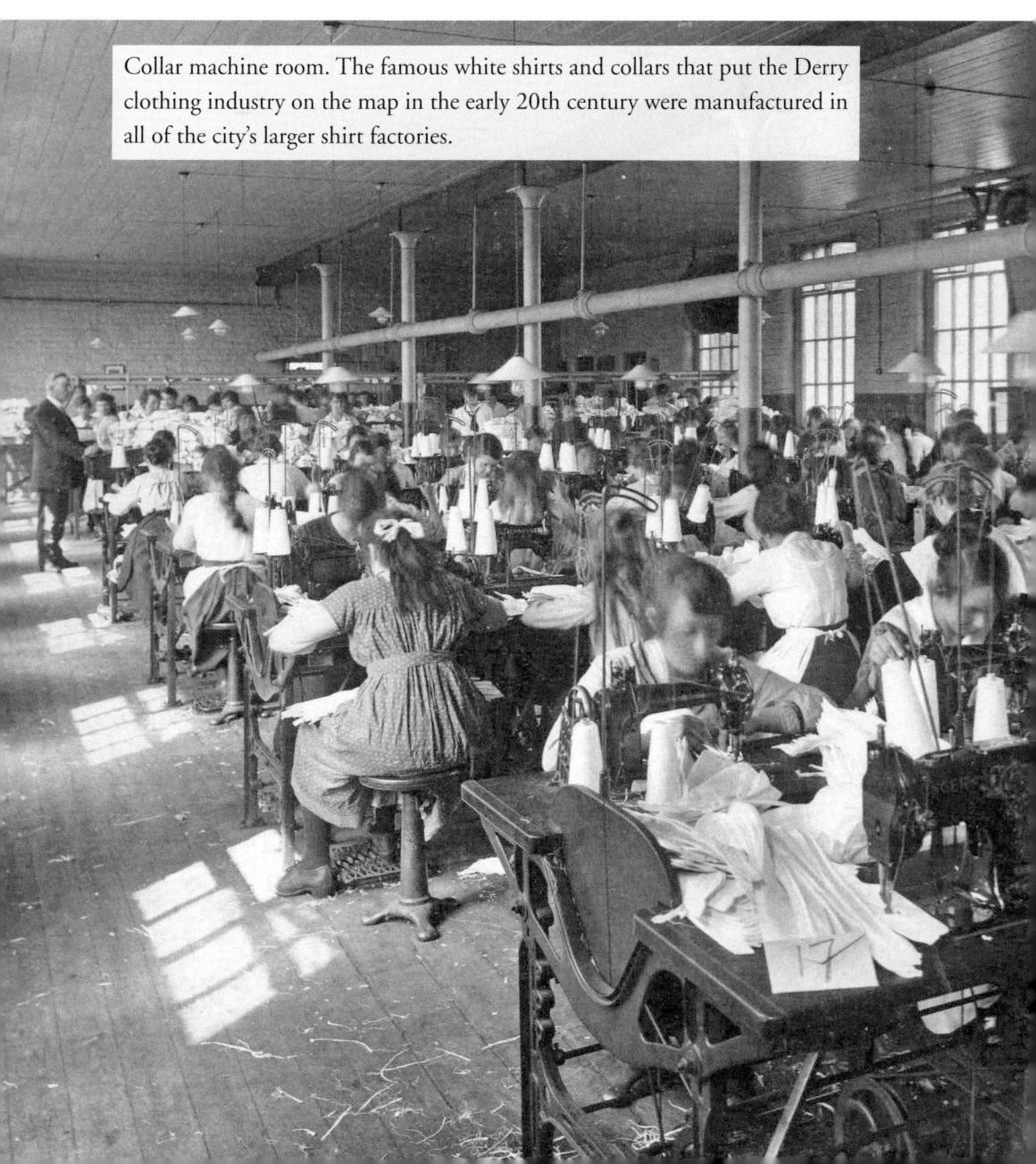

Collar machine room. The famous white shirts and collars that put the Derry clothing industry on the map in the early 20th century were manufactured in all of the city's larger shirt factories.

Girls hard at work in the collar laundry.

MC.INTYRE, HOGG, MARSH & CO.

The "Berlin" White Shirt.

The BERLIN SHIRT.

With Collar Attached.

Tillie and Henderson workers on the iron steps into the factory over Tillie's Brae.

Freddy Pigott, department manager of the City Factory, enjoying
a lighter moment with some of the workers.

Christmas factory party.

Tillie and Henderson's Christmas dance, with the factory management seated at front, circa 1960s.

A Welch Margetson Christmas dinner dance. Included: Molly Kelly,
Kathleen Campbell and Marie Kelly.

City Factory Christmas dance. From left: Mary
Clifford, Clare Bridge and Vera Sheerin.

City Factory girls enjoying their annual dance
in The Embassy. From left: Clare Bridge,
Helen Kelly and Agnes Loughery.

Welch Margetson Christmas dance in 1963.

Welch Margetson Christmas dance in 1963. Back, from left: Ruby Porter, Mrs Cruicshank, unknown, Patsy McLaughlin, unknown and Hazel Reynolds. Front, from left: Unknown, Mary Doherty, Mary White, Adrian Ross (manager), Bernie Meehan, Margaret McCreedy, Kathleen McCauley and Mrs Reynolds.

A City Factory retirement presentation for Mary Toland. Included: Mrs Steward, Ella Fitzpatrick, Roy Henderson (Managing Director) and Effie Fitzpatrick.

Enjoying the sun outside the City Factory. Included: Pat Mooney, May Lynch and Margaret Lynch.

The City Factory manager presents retirement gifts to Ella Fitzpatrick.

Experienced City Factory workers travelling to Liverpool and Manchester to share their skills with trainees in partner factories. From left: Peggy Grey, Rosaleen McKeogh, Betty Nicell, Meena Hamilton, Carmel Doherty, Bridie Doherty, Sadie Kydd, Vera Williamson, Kathleen Callaghan, Tess Houston and unknown.

Ann Ming and Kathleen Baron join some of their friends from the City Factory laundry section at a Hen Party.

Biker girls Marie Kelly, Frances Barr and Jean Bonner from Cedric Factory hit the road.

Taking a breath of fresh air at the door of Cedric's Factory. Included: Priscilla McGilloway, Bridie Donnelly, Frances Barr, Marie Kelly and Ann Bonner.

Below: Rosaline McCarron with some friends from Wilkinson's Factory on a break.

Left and below: Closing day of Lloyd, Attree & Smith Factory in Great James Street. Included: Willie Long, Isobel Wisher, Lally Dunne, Marie Kelly and Kathleen Duffy.

City Factory bus run refreshment stop at Letterkenny. Included: Margaret Lynch, Ann McDaid and Evelyn Doherty.

One of Mary Toland's annual bus runs from the City Factory. Back, from left: Bernadette Doherty, Veronica Doherty, Mary Doherty and Eilish Anderson. Front: Veronica Dunne and Rosemary Boyle.

Monica McDowell (left) and colleagues packing shirts at Richies Factory.

Rosemount Factory, 1920s.

Above: Stopping for tea, coffee and smokes on a Richies Factory outing.

Workers leaving Tillie and Henderson's by the iconic metal steps onto Craigavon Bridge in the early 1950s.

Ron Simpson, manager of the City Factory, with the winner of the City Factory Queen competition and event organisers.

Kathleen Cunningham (front) at work in the City Factory.

Factory Reunion Gallery

Many former shirt-factory workers reunited to celebrate the launch of *Tillies* by Patsy Durnin in the City Hotel in 2005. The Springhill Dance Orchestra, featuring the author and other well-known local musicians, entertained an enthusiastic audience on the night.

Patsy Durnin and members of the Springhill Dance Orchestra get the evening off to a swinging start at the launch.

Michael and Myra Lynch, Rosaleen and Gerry Brady, Bobby White
and Paddy Quinn. At back: Harry Harkin.

Cousins Harry and Bobby Coyle.

Trevor Temple, Maura Craig and Rosita Cunningham.

Tillies' author Patsy Durnin being presented with a brick
from the demolished factory by Professor Robert Gavin.

Above: Photo includes Stella McDaid, Berna McDermott, Roy and Gloria Turton, and Patsy Durnin.

Susie and Eamon McDowell.

Tom Mullan and friends.

Phyllis and John McCourt.

Maureen Fox, Sheila Molloy and Kathleen Gallagher.

Eithne Glackin and husband with Harry Coyle and friends.

Lily Hegarty and sister.

George Sweeney with wife and friends.

Danny Kelly, Bridie Doherty and daughter Margaret with friend.

George Sweeney and Tony Mullan.

Larry Doherty with Jim Canning and wife.

Maria Quigley and Don Harkin with friends.

Mickey Singh (in bow tie) and friends.

Eileen Hegarty joins her friends on the dance floor.

A smiling Mary Durnin.

Rose and Margaret O'Kane with friends.

Lyla Millar and Don O'Reilly.

Una Murray and Barney Watkins with friends.

Bobby O'Donnell and wife Bridie with Clare Henderson.

Clare Hughes, Mrs Anderson and Ginny Braid.

Margaret McCreedy and friends.

Kathleen and Hanna Quigley with Maura Wade and friends.

Tony Griffith and wife.

Philomena Concannon and friends.

Mura Ward with her sister and friends.

Frances Doherty (on left) with friends.

Lily Rankin and Ann Higgins with friends.

Bridie Sharkey with friends.

Rita McGuinness and Sheila Molloy.

John and Frances Doherty with Stella McDaid.

Enjoying the speeches. Photo includes local historian Michael McGuinness and wife Deta.